CHILDREN'S PRAYER MANUAL

Children's Illustrated Bible Study On Prayer (Ages 7-14 Years)

by

David Walters

Illustrated by Jessica Ellis Age 11

Graphics Design & Layout by Lisa-Joy Walters, and John Hester

Published by
GOOD NEWS FELLOWSHIP MINISTRIES
220 Sleepy Creek Rd.
Macon, GA 31210
Phone:(478)757-8071   Fax:(478)757-0136
e-mail: goodnews@reynoldscable.net
web site: goodnews.netministries.org
DavidWaltersMinistry.com
International Standard Book Number: 1-888081-62-7

Printed by : FAITH PRINTING
4210 Locust Hill Road
Taylors SC 29687

CHAPTER ONE

Children can do almost ANYTHING that adults do. They may not always be able to do it so well, but they can do a lot more than most of us think.

For example:

The young lad **David** slew the giant Goliath with a sling and a few pebbles!

Little **Samuel** received a message from God to tell his spiritual father, Eli, the high priest, that he and his family was going to be judged by God, because he have never disciplined his two sons who turned out bad!

John the Baptist was filled with the Holy Spirit even before he was born!

In the 1700"s *David Faraguet* an American navel officer joined the navy when he was nine and took command of a captured British vessel when he was twelve!

John Quincy Adams was a Ambassador to the Catherine the Great of Russia when he was fourteen!

The hymn writer *Francis Ridley Havergal* apparently could quote the whole of the New Testament and the book of Psalms by heart at the age of three. When she was five she could read the New Testament in the original Greek!

When the Celtic Christian **Cuthbert** was eight years old he <u>loved to play games and sports</u>. One day when he was playing he was challenged by a **three year old boy** to give his life to God and stop wasting his life playing sports. When Cuthbert laughed, the little child threw himself on the ground and began to weep.

This so affected Cuthbert that he eventually gave his life to God.

Today, children are beginning to pray, rather than just play,
<u>WITH AMAZING RESULTS!!</u>

THE 10/40 WINDOW?

Children's Global Prayer Movement has plans to enlist **two million children** to pray all over the world for people to accept Jesus, especially through the **10/40 window.**

What is the 10/40 window? It is an imaginary narrow window across part of the world where a lot of people don't know about or don't believe in Jesus. **It's a part of the world where millions of people believe in different religions, like Muslims, Hindu's, Buddhists, and others**. Since children have been praying, many of these people have found the Lord. Some Muslims have met Jesus in their dreams and He has told them that He is the Savior. Lots of other miracles have been happening and even some people are being raised from the dead.

Doesn't that make praying exciting??

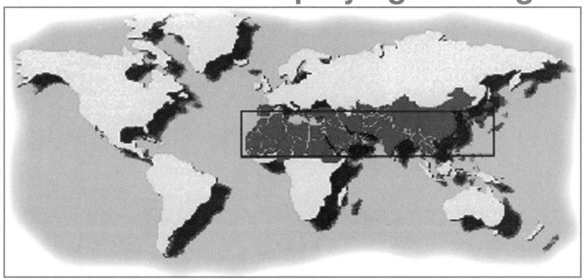

6

Everybody knows that kids love to play. In fact children can play for **hours and hours** and they don't mind getting hot and sweaty when they play so hard.

Why?

Because they are having such a good time!

But kids don't usually **pray** for hours and hours and get sweaty, because they are praying so hard. Yet this I believe is God's desire. I remember being at a children's camp where some of the kids began to pray. One boy about **TEN** began to pray out real loud to God and ask the Lord to forgive his sins and then he prayed even harder for the Lord to save his friends and some of his family. Two other kids watching him said, *"Wow! he's really getting into it."* <u>HE was</u>! God was really moving on him and he was doing some serious praying!

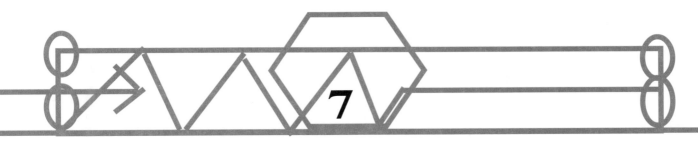

We have already seen that children are very good at playing.

In fact, **NOBODY CAN PLAY LIKE KIDS. They just love to play. We also know that they don't even mind getting hot and sweaty playing, as long as they are having a good time.**

Also kids don't like to play alone for too long, they love to play with their friends. In the same way kids will sometimes pray in a crowd at church when someone tells them to, **but they may not pray very much on their own or by themselves.**

I had a friend who worked for our ministry and *his eleven year old daughter would go into her bedroom every day and pray and spend time with God,* AND SHE LOVED TO DO IT.

A pastor friend of mine has a twelve year old son who loves to pray all the time and SHOWS UP FOR ALL THE CHURCH PRAYER MEETINGS.

I wonder if you have ever gotten hot and sweaty through praying? Some of you might say "Yes", because it was hot in the church or in my room. But what I mean is have you ever prayed so hard you sweated. You know Jesus prayed so hard once that He sweated great drops of blood. Wow! he must have really been praying. It was called the "The agony in the Garden." He was about to be betrayed by Judas and he cried to His father to give Him strength to do what he had to do. What did He have to do? He was to be crucified for our sins. To be arrested like a criminal and be killed was not something to look forward to. This was not going to be fun. I wonder if we would be willing to die and be covered in someone else's sin, especially if we disliked **them?**

○   When people go to church on Sunday morning, they usually see children running around playing and teenagers standing around talking before the service starts.

○ Sometimes a few church leaders and adults pray before the service, but **not** usually kids.

That's because we don't realize that God *wants* our children to pray and that their prayers **are very important and could make a tremendous difference to the church!**

I believe that the <u>children and the teens are the very ones that God wants to use to bring revival</u>.

Most adults would be blown away if they visited a church and saw kids and youth PRAYING AND INTERCEDING BEFORE THE SERVICE HAD STARTED, INSTEAD OF PLAYING AND TALKING.

<u>A lot of people would join that church and bring their kids if they saw that happening!!</u>

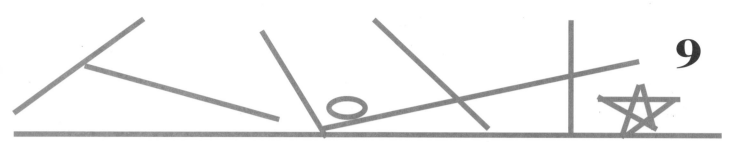
Like everything else you have to practice praying. The more you do it, the better you become. You also have to pray with your heart and mind on God and not just say prayers like a parrot. (You know! Praying without thinking, or praying while thinking about other things, or praying and not really meaning it.)

When you ask your parents for something you usually want to get their ATTENTION . So you get in their face, you want them to make eye contact with you and make them listen to what you have to say. I've heard kids call "Mom" about ten times, until their mother answers them.

Kids don't like being ignored by their parents or any adult for that matter, especially when they want something. Kids tend to keep bugging their parents until they get what they want. God does not mind us bugging Him, it's called persistent prayer, or diligently seeking Him.

When you pray to God, DON'T BE WHINY, VAGUE OR WIMPY, but be clear and precise and tell God what you need.

"Let us therefore come boldly to the throne of grace, that we may obtain mercy and find grace to help in time of need" **(Heb.4:16).**

I've seen little kids fall down and hurt themselves and then run to their parents screaming. *The parents want to know what the matter is,* but the child is too **stressed out** to make sense. The kid is screaming and sobbing so bad that he can't let them know where he is hurting. The parents have to calm down the child enough to tell them the problem and only then can they do something about it. **How can you kiss the Boo Boo and make it better when you don't know where it is?**

Some adults pray to God like a screaming and sobbing kid, *HOPING* that they will get His attention so He will respond. I believe that GOD DOES NOT WANT US TO PRAY TO HIM CRYING, SCREAMING AND SOBBING, but to pray in faith with confidence, believing that He will answer our prayers.

That's what I believe the scripture we just quoted means (see Heb.4:16).

Remember prayer is talking to your heavenly Father. Don't be in too much of a hurry. Wait for Him to answer you. Be willing to wait and listen. Some people just burst out a lot of words to God and run off before He can answer them.

Lots of kids tend to be impatient and can't wait for things. Don't be like that with God.
"Be still and know that I am God." **Psalm 46:10** *"They that wait upon the lord shall renew their strength."* **Isaiah 40:31**

How should YOU pray?

Kneeling Down, Standing Up, Sitting Up, Lying down? You can pray **any** of these ways, it doesn't matter as long as you mean it. Sometimes when you think of God as the mighty Lord and King it would be good to *kneel* or *fall on your face*. Other times, you might think of Him as your Daddy and you can pray to Him when your'e lying in your bed, LIKE WHEN PARENTS COME TO TUCK THEIR KIDS IN AND KISS THEM GOODNIGHT.

Then you can pray to Jesus when you are walking along and remembering Him as friend and brother. In fact **you can pray anytime**, even when you're playing games, taking a shower, or even sitting on the potty

When Jesus taught His Disciples how to pray He taught them the Lord's prayer:

"Our Father who is in heaven, Holy is your name, Let your kingdom come, let Your will be done on earth, as it is in heaven. Give us daily our food, take care of our needs and forgive us when we sin, as we forgive people that sin against us. Don't allow us to be led into temptation, but keep us from evil, for Yours is the kingdom and the power and the glory for ever and ever, Amen" (Matt 6:9).

Although it is good for kids and adults to learn the Lord's prayer by heart and recite it everyday, it was given by Jesus for more than doing just that. He was showing us the best way to pray in the right order. He was showing us how to approach or come to God.
He then shows us how to bring our needs to God, and then shows us how to finish our prayers.

LET'S LOOK AT THE LORD'S PRAYER MORE CLOSELY

<u>**1. Our Father who is in heaven, Holy is your name**</u>. This reminds us that God is our heavenly Father or Dad, but He is also Holy. In other words we thank God first for being our Father. Remember He is not everyone's Father, but only to those who have received His Son into their hearts and lives. God is the creator of everyone, but because He is the creator it does not make Him everyone's Father. Only when we become Christians and accept Jesus into our hearts and lives He becomes our Father. Then we talk to Him with respect and honor because, He is HOLY!

He is Holy! It is more important to be in God's presence than standing before the President of the United States of America. or some great King of some great country. One day, **all the kings of the earth will lay their crowns down before our Lord.**

2. Your Kingdom come. Your will be done on earth as it is in heaven.

Jesus reminds us that **GOD'S KINGDOM IS MORE IMPORTANT THAN THIS WORLD**. So TOYS, MOVIES, T.V., SCHOOL, FRIENDS, and other things, should **not** take more of our time and interest than GOD AND HIS KINGDOM.

We are also to pray first that God's will is done on this earth. That means the devil will finally be defeated and God will soon reign over everyone on this earth like He does in heaven.

Part of God's will is that

all people should be saved and none should perish.

This means He wants us not only to pray for lost people in different places and countries, but also tell our friends, neighbors and family about Jesus and win them for <u>Him.</u>

3. Give us this day our daily bread. OUR HEAVENLY FATHER LIKES US TO REMEMBER THAT **HE** IS THE ONE THAT SUPPLIES OUR NEEDS. HE SENDS THE **RAIN** AND THE **SUN** SO OUR CROPS WILL GROW. WHAT ARE CROPS? **VEGETABLES, FRUIT**, AND ALSO **CORN, WHEAT AND BARLEY,** WHICH GIVES YOU YOUR BREAKFAST CERERAL.

> **H**E ALSO GIVES YOUR DAD STRENGTH TO GO TO WORK AND EARN MONEY **A**ND YOUR MOM STRENGTH TO TAKE CARE OF YOU. **S**O WE SHOULD ASK **H**IM EVERY DAY TO TAKE CARE OF THESE THINGS AND PROTECT US AND THOSE THAT WE LOVE. **S**OME KIDS SAY THEY DON'T KNOW WHAT TO PRAY FOR, IT'S PROBABLY BECAUSE THEY DON'T REALLY UNDERSTAND THE **L**ORD'S PRAYER.

WE ARE NOW BEGINNING TO SEE THAT THERE ARE PLENTY OF THINGS TO PRAY FOR. REMEMBER TO HAVE REGULAR PRAYER. PRAY EVERY DAY. YOU DON'T FORGET TO EAT EVERY DAY, SO DON'T FORGET TO PRAY. MAKE A SPECIAL TIME TO SPEND WITH THE LORD. IT'S GOOD TO GET UP EXTRA EARLY SO YOU CAN START YOUR DAY RIGHT WITH PRAYER...

THINGS HAVE A HABIT OF GOING BETTER FOR US WHEN WE START THE DAY TALKING TO GOD.

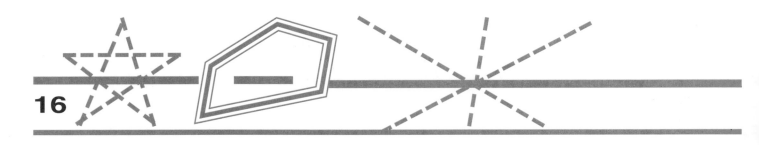

4. And forgive us our sins as we forgive people that sin against us. *Sometimes we commit sin.* That means we decide to do something wrong or bad or behave in a wrong or bad way, even though we are **Christians**.

Other times we kind of just fall into sin. We do something bad or wrong without thinking. We lose our temper, be mean to someone, be disobedient to our parents or teachers, or get involved with kids that don't love God and they influence us to behave badly.

If these kind of things happen, we need to <u>repent and tell God we are truely sorry.</u>

If people do bad things to us we need to FORGIVE THEM QUICKLY. If we hold grudges against people and won't forgive them, how do we expect God to forgive us our sins. We have offended God much more than people have offended us.

The two pictures on page sixteen and the picture above tell the story from the Bible about the unjust servant. He owed the king a million dollars, but he couldn't pay his debt. This meant that all his family would be sold into slavery and his possessions taken away. So he begged the king to give him time to repay him. The king then felt sorry for him and forgave him his debt.

Then the servant went to a fellow servant who owed him fifty dollars and demanded that he pay him. The servant said, "Please give me time to pay you." But he wouldn't and threw him in jail, took his house and all his possessions. *When the king found out what the bad servant had done he was very angry and had him tortured until he paid the million dollars back. (see Matt 18:23-35)*

SO REMEMBER, IF WE DON'T FORGIVE PEOPLE, HOW DO WE EXPECT GOD TO FORGIVE US?

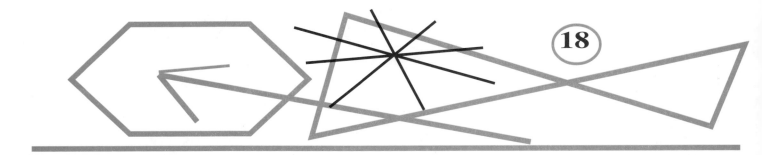

5. Lead us not into temptation, but deliver us from evil.

This is a very important prayer that we need to pray every day. The devil is out to get us. He is the one who tempts us and he uses his demons to mess us up, especially if we go into certain areas.

Ask God to deliver you from being tempted to hang out with the wrong crowd or play with the wrong kind of kids. If you make a bad kid your best friend, then the devil will use him or her to tempt you to become bad also. Ask God to help you find good friends, who love the Lord and will be an encouragment to you to go on with the Lord. Pray to the Lord every day and ask Him to guide your steps, so you can walk in His ways and not your own ways. You should be friendly to bad or unsaved kids so you can talk them about Jesus and lead them to the Lord,

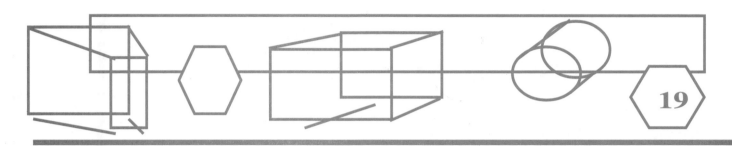
But don't make them your best friends unless they get radically saved. If you fall into temptation, confess your sin and ask God to forgive you, then also ask God to keep you from falling into temptation again.

"Now to Him who is able to keep you from falling or stumbling, and present you faultless before the presence of His glory with exceeding joy." (Jude 24).

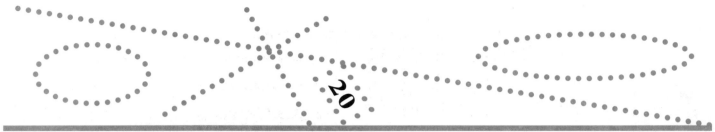

6. For Yours is the kingdom and the power and the glory for ever and ever amen.

Now Jesus reminds us after we have asked God to meet our needs and help us, we need to

FINISH OUR PRAYING BY GIVING OUR HEAVENLY FATHER THE GLORY HE DESERVES.

Tell God how awesome He is and how awesome His kingdom is. A lot of you kids have heard or sung the song "Our God is an awesome God."
Well sing it again and really mean it and give our God the glory.

You know the Bible says that one day all the whole world is going to see the glory of God and all the kings and all the nations shall bow before Him.

"That at the name of <u>Jesus</u> every knee should bow, of those in heaven, and those on earth, and those under the earth, and that every tongue should confess that Jesus is Lord, TO THE GLORY OF GOD THE FATHER." (Phil. 2:10)

 Hearing God's voice is very important. God does speak to us and when we pray we must remember not to do all the talking, but give God a chance to answer. Also we should learn to be sensitive so the Lord can talk to us anytime and we will listen*!*

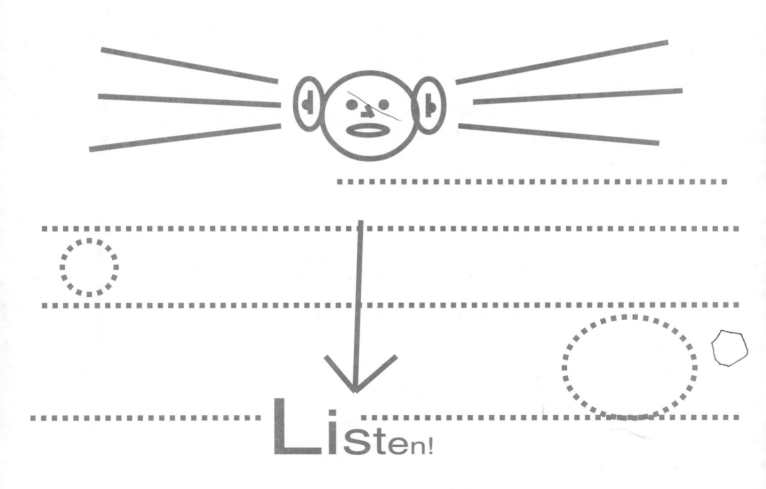

Listen!

1. God can speak in an audible voice. That means He talks in a voice that we can hear with our ears. This has happened a number times in the Bible. Here are a few examples that you can check out:

God talked to Moses out of a bush.(See Ex.3:4.) God called young Samuel when he was just a kid and Samuel thought it was Eli the priest calling him. (See 1.Sam.3:4-9.)

God talked out loud from heaven when Jesus was with his disciples on the mount of transfiguration. **"This is my beloved Son: hear Him"** (Mark 9:7).

God called down from heaven and spoke to Saul when he was persecuting the Christians, and Saul fell of his horse, and became the great Apostle Paul. The others with him heard the voice, but saw no one and were amazed. (See Acts 9:4-7.)

HERE IS ANOTHER STORY OF JESUS PRAYING IN PUBLIC.

"Father glorify Your name." Then a voice came from heaven, saying, "I have both glorified it and will glorify it again." Therefore the people who stood by and heard it said that it had thundered. Others said, "An angel has spoken to Him."
(John.12:28-29).

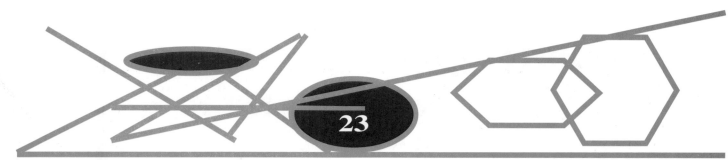

Now don't make the mistake of thinking that unless God speaks to you like that, you will never hear His voice. I believe that <u>God can still speak that way and a number of people have claimed to hear Him speak to them in an audible voice, so it could happen to you.</u>

> **But it is more likely that God will speak to you in other ways.**

2.God speaks to us through His word (the scriptures.)

God has given us the Bible so that we can know His will for us. If we don't bother to read His word, then we can't know His will and we won't know how to <u>live</u> as a Christian. If we read the Bible everyday, faithfully believing that God will speak to us and show us things,

IT WILL HAPPEN!

It's like digging for gold. You can't just dig for a few minutes and then get tired or bored and expect to find gold.

> **You have to keep at it, persevere, not give up easily, and then it will happen.**

As you do this, you will often find that a certain passage or verse of scripture will kind of jump out at you and you will know that it is for <u>YOU.</u>

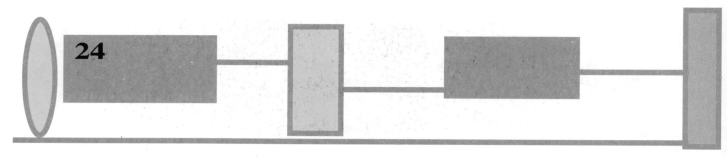

It's like reading something that you have read before many times, but God suddenly speaks to you through that verse and you say, "Wow! I've never really seen or understood that before." And you take it, knowing that God has given it especially for you.

That's known as the "Rhema" word, which means the "proceeding" word. It's coming fresh from God's mouth direct to you. The Bible is the "Logas" word, that's the word that God has said in the beginning and has been written in the Bible. So when a scripture kind of **jumps** out at you, the Logas becomes the Rhema. God speaks **the written word to your heart especially for you. Some people have said that the Bible is God's love letter to us.**

3.God speaks to our hearts.

SPEAK

If we spend time with God and are willing to be quiet. He will speak to our hearts. In the Bible, it's called the STILL SMALL VOICE OF GOD. (See 1. Kings 19:11-13)

Spending time like this with God is especially challenging to KIDS. People tell us that kids are too busy playing and running around to be quiet and spend time with God, so they don't usually encourage kids or expect them to do it.

But..... God expects them to, and I believe that kids can do this really well, if they put their mind and heart into it. I don't mean that you have to spend your whole life seeking God and you never have anytime to play. I mean that you can practice getting into His presence everyday. You might start out with only five or ten minutes, but the more you put your heart into it, the longer it will get. You could end up spending a half an hour or even an hour with God, but it will be so good listening to Him, that it will seem like only a few minutes!

How **does** God speak to our hearts? WELL, HIS VOICE DOES NOT ALWAYS COME IN AN AUDIBLE WAY, BUT HE WILL TELL YOU THINGS AND THEY WILL COME INTO YOUR THOUGHTS. *How do you know they are from God and they are not just your imagination?* Well you won't know at first, but as you PRACTICE LISTENING, you will learn to tell the difference between just your thoughts and God's.

4. God speaks to us through people.

Always be ready to listen to the preacher, whether it's your Pastor, a visiting minister, or your Sunday school teacher. Also listen to your parents. God has given us Christian parents to train us and help us grow in God. Don't play around at church and talk to other kids and distract them from hearing God's word being preached. When you go to church, don't say, "THIS ISN'T FOR ME, THIS IS FOR GROWN UPS."SAY "LORD I KNOW I AM JUST A KID, BUT YOU WANT TO TALK TO ME AND TELL ME THINGS I NEED TO KNOW, SO I AM GOING TO PAY ATTENTION AND LISTEN AND HAVE MY HEART OPEN TO RECEIVE FROM YOU."

GOD SOMETIMES SPEAKS TO US THROUGH NON-CHRISTIANS. FOR EXAMPLE, YOU COULD BE FOOLING AROUND AT SCHOOL AND NOT BEHAVING LIKE A CHRISTIAN SHOULD AND SOME KID COMES UP AND SAYS, "I THOUGHT YOU'RE SUPPOSED TO BE A CHRISTIAN?" THEN YOU FEEL GUILTY AND ASHAMED THAT YOU HAVE NOT BEEN A GOOD WITNESS FOR THE LORD. GOD COULD BE WARNING YOU TO STRAIGHTEN UP AND IS USING A NON-CHRISTIAN TO SPEAK TO YOU!

5. <u>God speaks to us through our circumstances.</u> *What does that mean?*

Well Imagine your parents tell you not to play in a certain place, because it's dangerous. But you disobey and do it and nothing happens. So you think you can keep on playing in that place, even though your parents told you not to. Then some time later you go and play and you get hurt, because it was dangerous and you end up in the hospital. Then your parents come and say,

I"ve told you so, I hope you have learned your lesson."

So you learned the hard way.

If we keep on disobeying God and will not listen to Him when he speaks to our hearts, or through other people, and we will not read His word, then HE MAY SPEAKS TO US THROUGH CIRCUMSTANCES IN ORDER TO GET OUR ATTENTION. He allows the devil to jump on us, because we have been disobedient and have come out from under His protection. WE HAVE BEEN REBELLIOUS AND DID WHAT WE WANTED, RATHER THAT WHAT HE WANTED. SO THEN SOMETHING BAD HAPPENS TO US AND THAT MAKES US REPENT AND BE SORRY.

From The Bible...

. . .Absalom sent for Joab to send him to the king, but he would not come to him. And when he sent again a second time, he would not come. So Absalom said to his servants, "See Joab's field is near mine, and he has barley there; go set it on fire." And Absalom's servants set the field on fire. Then Joab arose and came to Absalom and said to him, "Why have your servants set my fields on fire?" And Absalom answered Jaob, "Look I sent to you saying , 'Come here, so that I can send you to the king...." (2.Sam.14:29-32).

GOD SPEAKS THROUGH CIRCUMSTANCES!!

In that scripture story you just read, Joab was too busy doing his own thing to come when he was called, so Absalom set fire to his barely field to get his attention. IT WORKED, Joab came running and asked Absalom why he did that. He told him, "I called you twice and you would not listen, so now I've got your attention."

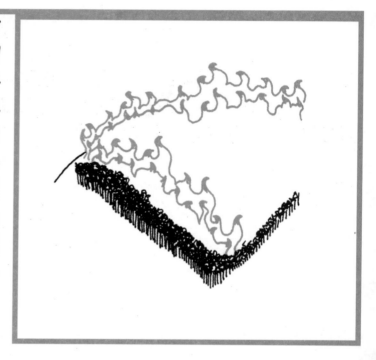

You say, "I don't have any barley fields." But EVERYBODY has things that are important to them. It could be a bike, or a pet, or a computer, or toy, that you cherish. I don't want to scare you, but be careful that you don't get so busy with your things, that God allows the devil to take some of them away to get your attention. IT'S BETTER TO HEAR GOD SPEAK TO US IN THE OTHER WAYS WE HAVE MENTIONED, than to have to speak to us through our circumstances. Even dads can sometimes get so busy working that they don't have time to go to church or seek God and then they wonder why they get sick and lose all their money and why things are not working out for them. *Remember the Bible says that if we put God first and His kingdom then He will take care of all our other needs. (See Matt.6:33)*

Some Kids say that JESUS IS THEIR BEST FRIEND, but don't know much about Him. Do you call Jesus your best friend? Well if you do, you had better make sure you know him. **I HAVE NEVER MET A KID WHO SAYS HE HAS A BEST FRIEND, BUT HARDLY EVER TALKS TO HIM AND DOESN'T EVEN KNOW WHERE HE LIVES.**

He doesn't know his telephone number, what his favorite games and sports are, his nickname, what he like to eat, or how many brothers or sisters he has. When you have a best friend, you hang out together and call each other up and talk. *Girls do that all the time.* Well you will never know Jesus as your best friend, unless you

SPEND TIME WITH HIM AND TALK AND LISTEN TO HIM.

Also you would not take your best friend to bad or dangerous places. You should never go anywhere or run around with anyone if you are ashamed to take Jesus along with you. Remember, **He is supposed to be your best friend.**

Lots of parents let their kids do what they like. Other parents only get their children to obey them after they have told them to do something FIVE OR SIX TIMES! Some children only obey their parents when they get mad and start screaming at them. Lots of parents argue with their kids about cleaning their rooms, taking out the trash, stop teasing their baby sister etc. So the kid only obeys when they are really mad. Then the child thinks that God is like that. They think you can continually be disobedient and sinful, until finally God gets mad and then you straighten up for a while. But then you go back and do it again.

This is bad training from the parents. Parents should expect their children to obey them the first time they ask them to do something. If kids disobey they should be punished right away with no second chance. This is not because we want parents to be mean to you kids, but to train you up to be how God wants you to be. If you don't learn to listen and obey your parents voice, you will not learn to hear and obey the voice of God.

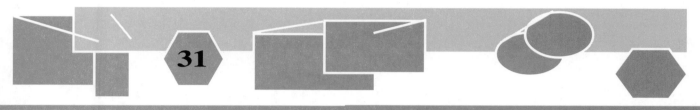

When little Samuel heard God calling Him he thought it was Eli the priest. (He was living with Eli who was like his stepfather.) Remember Samuel was in bed nice and cozy, but as soon as he heard a voice calling him, he jumped out of bed and **ran** over to Eli and asked him what he wanted. Eli said he did not call him and told him to go back to bed. This happened three times until Eli realized that God was calling Samuel. He then told Samuel to tell the Lord to speak to Him when he called Him and tell God that he was listening.

"...The Lord called Samuel. And he answered 'Here I am!' So he ran to Eli and said, 'Here I am, for you called me' And he said 'I did not call, lie down again. And he went and lay down. And the Lord called yet again, 'Samuel' So Samuel arose and went to Eli and said, 'Here I am, you called me.' And he answered, 'I did not call, my son, lie down again.' (Now Samuel did not know the Lord, nor was the word of the Lord yet revealed to him) And the Lord called Samuel again a third time. Then he arose and went to Eli and said, 'Here I am for you called me.' Then Eli perceived that the Lord had called the boy. Therefore Eli said to Samuel, 'Go lie down; and it shall be, if He calls you, that you must say, 'Speak Lord, for your servant hears.' So Samuel went down and lay in his place. (bed) Then the Lord stood and called as at the other times, 'Samuel, Samuel' and Samuel answered, 'Speak for Your Servant hears.'" **(1.Sam.3:4-10)**

If you want to hear the voice of God like Samuel, you must learn to obey your parents the first time they call you. When you are warm and cozy in bed and your Mom calls and says, "Come on it's time to get up for school. "Remember, if she has to call you more than once, then both of you are making a big mistake and she is not teaching you how to hear and obey the voice of God.

CHAPTER SIX

Praying in public or praying for kids and adults in church services should be easy for children to do. The **most important thing is to receive God's anointing.** That means make sure you are filled with the Holy Spirit and you are allowing Him to use, lead, and control you. The best kind of prayer is that which is INSPIRED by the *Holy Spirit*. If our praying is prompted by God, then we know it started in heaven where God dwells, comes to earth, flows through us, and then goes back into heaven. **That's the kind of prayer which <u>really</u> works.**

We have to *PRACTICE* at praying in public. Some churches might not like children praying for people in case they mess up, so kids don't get the opportunity to try. If you are allowed to pray, and it doesn't always seem to work, don't give up. WE LEARN BY OUR MISTAKES. Some kids are frightened to pray for people in case it doesn't work, but unless you try you will never know. Often in my meetings many of the children and youth are touched

by the Spirit of God. I then have them pray for people in our Sunday evening miracle services. I call it, <u>"The laying on of sticky fingers."</u> We have seen a lot of people receive healing through **the ministry of children and youth.** Many people that have been in pain for years are instantly healed. People who are deaf have been able to hear again. Several people with one blind eye have seen perfectly. Even some crippled people have walked again. Although some church leaders and some parents may have a problem with children praying in church for adults, **GOD DOESN'T.**

I remember being in one church meeting and I was praying and prophesying over some people when a boy about eleven years old jumped up and began to do the same as me. He prayed and prophesied over children and adults for about half an hour. When he finally stopped he said to me,

"I've never done that before. I've never prayed in public and prophesied before; especially over big people. "How come I did that?" "You didn't, it wasn't you" I replied. "If I didn't, who did it then?" he said. "It was the Holy Spirit!" I replied. "It was?" He exclaimed, He thought for a moment and then said, "Wow!"

The Holy Spirit had taken over and used that eleven year old boy to pray and prophesy, because he had been obedient to the leading of the Holy Spirit. Was able to do things which he normally couldn't do.

ZOE PRAYING FOR THE MAN TO GET OUT OF THE WHEELCHAIR!

In another meeting little eight year old Zoe had just been filled with the Holy Spirit. She came down from the meeting we had for children and saw the adults coming out from their meeting. She saw a man in a wheelchair and went over to him. She prayed to the Lord and He told her He wanted to heal the man, so she laid her hands on him and said,

"IN THE NAME OF JESUS GET OUT OF YOURWHEEL CHAIR."

In a moment the man jumped out and began walking. He had been crippled for six years!

A number of years later, I met a pastor who was the brother of the man who jumped out of the wheelchair, The pastor told me that his brother was still healed!

A ten year old boy was attending a conference I was speaking at, when the Lord spoke to him and said the following. "I want you to witness to all the kids in your school, all the kids in your neighborhood, all the kids in your town and then I will send you to be a missionary." Two years later, when he was twelve, he came back to another conference I was speaking at. I found out from His parents that he had led over 100 children to the Lord!

When you pray in public, be **BOLD** with your prayers. Some kids just lay their hands on people and just look around with a blank face. Don't be like that. Other kids ask God or Jesus to heal the people. He has told us to do it, not in our own power, but with His power. So when you pray for someone, be bold and say something like, " I take authority over this sickness (name the sickness). In Jesus name be healed and receive your miracle."

THEN EXPECT IT TO HAPPEN AND TELL THE PERSON TO ACT THEIR FAITH.

If they have pain in their body tell them to move their body where they hurt, pray in Jesus name and let the pain go. Also pray for people who need a job, or money to pay their bills, or want their kids, husband or wife, to be saved. Ask them if they have any need at all and you will pray for them. You can also lay hand on those that need a fresh touch of the Holy Spirit. pray for them and believe that God will touch them. You see, JESUS WANTS TO USE YOUR HANDS TO BLESS PEOPLE WITH AND ALL YOU HAVE TO DO IS BE SERIOUS AND YIELD TO HIM AND HE WILL FLOW THROUGH YOU WITH HIS ANOINTING.

I was recently having children praying in a meeting and a little girl about four or five years old was praying for an adult. She was praying in English and then in tongues. She prayed for God to touch that person and receive their deliverance and then said, "You are now free walk in your deliverance."

If a four or five year old can do that using the prayer of faith, what do you think you can do?

What does the Bible say?

"Evening and morning and at noon I will pray, and cry aloud, and He shall hear my voice" **(Ps 55.17) (NKJ)** It's good to pray three times a day. When you get up, when you have your lunch and when you go to bed.

"Pray for them which despitefully use you" **(Matt.5:44).**
That means we should pray for our enemies and kids that don't like us and are mean to us.

". . . pray to the Lord of the harvest to send laborers into His harvest." **(Luke 10:2)**
this means pray to the Lord to save our friends and to help us and raise up other young people to preach the gospel and **become soul winners**

"Watch and pray, lest you enter into temptation. The spirit truly is willing, but the flesh is weak." (Mark.14:38).
That means keep alert and pray and don't let the devil sneak up on you and make you fall into temptation and sin.

Also don't only pray when you feel like it. Learn to pray even when you're not in the mood for praying and God will bless you and the feelings to pray will come.

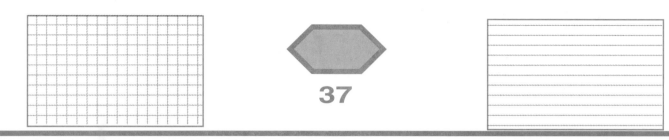

> *"Therefore I say to you, whatever things you ask when you pray, believe that you receive them, and you will have them"* **(Mk.11.24).**

This means you must believe you receive the answer when you pray. Most people believe that God answers their prayers when the result comes, but that's not faith. Imagine that you ask God to save your uncle and then say, I prayed now I am going to wait to see if God will do it and when He does I will believe. That's no good.

YOU MUST BELIEVE THAT GOD ANSWERED YOU WHEN YOU PRAYED, SO YOU THEN THANK GOD FOR SAVING HIM EVEN THOUGH YOU DON'T NECESSARILY SEE A CHANGE IN YOUR UNCLE RIGHT AWAY.

That's how my mom and dad got saved and my wife's mom. When we prayed for my wife's mom, she got worse and was not interested in Jesus, but we kept believing and thanking God that she was saved. After about three months she phoned and asked if she could come to church with us and that was it. SHE NEVER MISSED ANOTHER SUNDAY AND REALLY SERVED THE LORD!

"Men always ought to pray" **(Lk.18:1).**
That means we should be in the habit of praying. Prayer should come easy so we are able to pray at anytime. If an emergency happens, pray. We were at a church and God touched some kids of the song leader. He set them on fire for HIM. The next day their mother accidently backed the car over their baby brother. The little boy wasn't breathing and the parents began to panic. The children said, Lets pray and laid their hands on their baby brother and he began to breath. When they took him to the hospital to check him out he was ok. THE DOCTOR SAID IT WAS A MIRACLE. THE PARENTS SAID THEY BELIEVED THE CHILDREN WERE USED TO SAVE THEIR BABY'S LIFE.

"I make mention of you in my prayers" **(Rom.1:9).**
That's remembering others and their needs when we pray.

"IN EVERYTHING BY PRAYER" **(Phil 4:6).**
That means not to be anxious but take everything to God in prayer with a thankful heart.

"Praying with all prayer" **(Eph.6:18).**
That means praying powerfully and not praying wimpy or half hearted prayers.

"Prayer of faith shall save the sick....". **(James.5:15).**
That means when you pray in faith believing for the sick to be healed the Lord will answer the prayer.

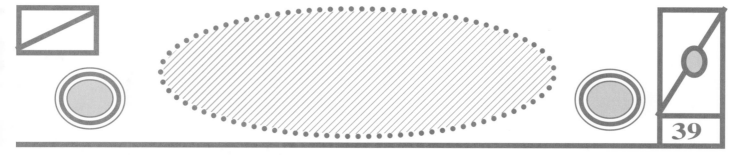

**"Praying always in the Spirit"** **(Eph.6:18)**

And

**"Praying in the Holy Ghost"** **(Jude 20)**

Here are some possible meanings to those two verses:

1. Praying in the power of the Spirit.
2. Praying prayers that are Spirit led or inspired by the Holy Spirit
3. Praying in other tongues or a heavenly language.

"Night and day praying exceedingly that we may see your face and perfect what is lacking in your faith" **(1.Thes.3.:10)**

Praying anytime, because God never sleeps.

WHY DON'T WE DO A PRAYER LOG?!

"What's a prayer log?"

With so much to pray for, let's make a prayer list and then we can write it down.
IT WILL BE EXCITING TO SEE HOW GOD ANSWERS PRAYER.

Below is an **example** of a prayer log

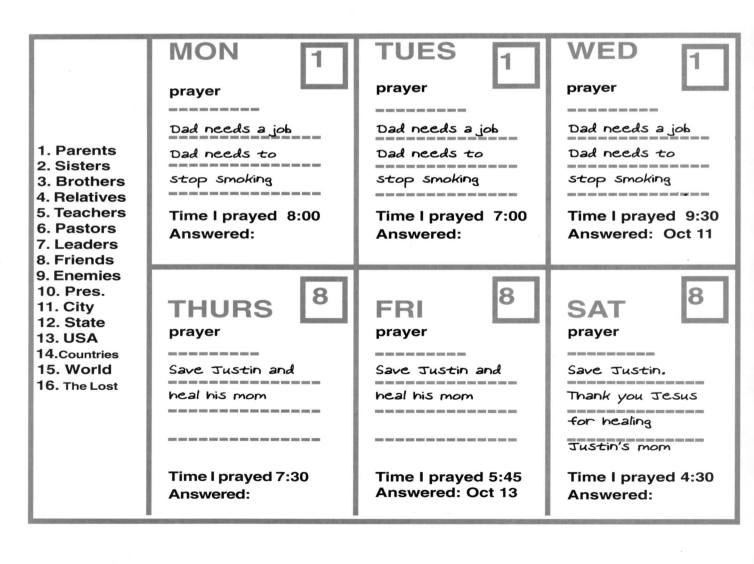

1. Parents
2. Sisters
3. Brothers
4. Relatives
5. Teachers
6. Pastors
7. Leaders
8. Friends
9. Enemies
10. Pres.
11. City
12. State
13. USA
14. Countries
15. World
16. The Lost

MON [1]

prayer
- - - - - - - - -
Dad needs a job
Dad needs to
stop smoking

Time I prayed 8:00
Answered:

TUES [1]

prayer
- - - - - - - - -
Dad needs a job
Dad needs to
stop smoking

Time I prayed 7:00
Answered:

WED [1]

prayer
- - - - - - - - -
Dad needs a job
Dad needs to
stop smoking

Time I prayed 9:30
Answered: Oct 11

THURS [8]

prayer
- - - - - - - - -
Save Justin and
heal his mom

Time I prayed 7:30
Answered:

FRI [8]

prayer
- - - - - - - - -
Save Justin and
heal his mom

Time I prayed 5:45
Answered: Oct 13

SAT [8]

prayer
- - - - - - - - -
Save Justin.
Thank you Jesus
for healing
Justin's mom

Time I prayed 4:30
Answered:

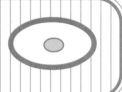

Make Copies As Needed

Numbers to Use

1. Parents
2. Sisters
3. Brothers
4. Relatives
5. Teachers
6. Pastors
7. Leaders
8. Friends
9. Enemies
10. President
11. City
12. State
13. USA
14. Countries
15. World
16. The Lost

MON
Prayer

Time I prayed
Answered

TUES
Prayer

Time I prayed
Answered

WED
Prayer

Time I prayed
Answered

THURS
Prayer

Time I prayed
Answered

FRI
Prayer

Time I prayed
Answered

SAT
Prayer

Time I prayed
Answered

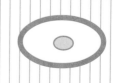

42

Make Copies As Needed

Numbers to Use			

Numbers to Use

1. Parents
2. Sisters
3. Brothers
4. Relatives
5. Teachers
6. Pastors
7. Leaders
8. Friends
9. Enemies
10. President
11. City
12. State
13. USA
14. Countries
15. World
16. The Lost

MON
Prayer

Time I prayed
Answered

TUES
Prayer

Time I prayed
Answered

WED
Prayer

Time I prayed
Answered

THURS
Prayer

Time I prayed
Answered

FRI
Prayer

Time I prayed
Answered

SAT
Prayer

Time I prayed
Answered

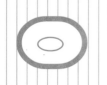
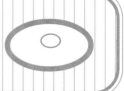

Make Copies As Needed

Numbers to Use

1. Parents
2. Sisters
3. Brothers
4. Relatives
5. Teachers
6. Pastors
7. Leaders
8. Friends
9. Enemies
10. President
11. City
12. State
13. USA
14. Countries
15. World
16. The Lost

MON
Prayer

Time I prayed
Answered

TUES
Prayer

Time I prayed
Answered

WED
Prayer

Time I prayed
Answered

THURS
Prayer

Time I prayed
Answered

FRI
Prayer

Time I prayed
Answered

SAT
Prayer

Time I prayed
Answered

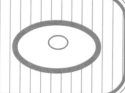

44

Make Copies As Needed

Numbers to Use

1. Parents
2. Sisters
3. Brothers
4. Relatives
5. Teachers
6. Pastors
7. Leaders
8. Friends
9. Enemies
10. President
11. City
12. State
13. USA
14. Countries
15. World
16. The Lost

MON
Prayer

Time I prayed
Answered

TUES
Prayer

Time I prayed
Answered

WED
Prayer

Time I prayed
Answered

THURS
Prayer

Time I prayed
Answered

FRI
Prayer

Time I prayed
Answered

SAT
Prayer

Time I prayed
Answered

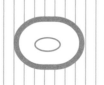
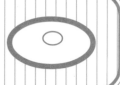

45

Make Copies As Needed

Numbers to Use

1. Parents
2. Sisters
3. Brothers
4. Relatives
5. Teachers
6. Pastors
7. Leaders
8. Friends
9. Enemies
10. President
11. City
12. State
13. USA
14. Countries
15. World
16. The Lost

MON
Prayer

———————
————————————
————————————
————————————
————————————
————————————
————————————
————————————

Time I prayed
Answered

TUES
Prayer

————————
————————————
————————————
————————————
————————————
————————————
————————————
————————————

Time I prayed
Answered

WED
Prayer

————————
————————————
————————————
————————————
————————————
————————————
————————————
————————————

Time I prayed
Answered

THURS
Prayer

————————
————————————
————————————
————————————
————————————
————————————
————————————
————————————

Time I prayed
Answered

FRI
Prayer

————————
————————————
————————————
————————————
————————————
————————————
————————————
————————————

Time I prayed
Answered

SAT
Prayer

————————
————————————
————————————
————————————
————————————
————————————
————————————
————————————

Time I prayed
Answered

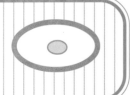

Make Copies As Needed

Numbers to Use

1. Parents
2. Sisters
3. Brothers
4. Relatives
5. Teachers
6. Pastors
7. Leaders
8. Friends
9. Enemies
10. President
11. City
12. State
13. USA
14. Countries
15. World
16. The Lost

MON
Prayer

Time I prayed
Answered

TUES
Prayer

Time I prayed
Answered

WED
Prayer

Time I prayed
Answered

THURS
Prayer

Time I prayed
Answered

FRI
Prayer

Time I prayed
Answered

SAT
Prayer

Time I prayed
Answered

"A Spiritual Encounter"

Reaching the Children
and Youth of the World
with Signs and Wonders.

Raising A Generation Of Anointed Children And Youth
and
Equipping The Younger Saints

The Ministry of Good News

SPECIAL FAMILY WEEKEND
PLUS A ONE DAY TRAINING SEMINAR

Equipping Youth Pastors, Sunday School Teachers, Children's Workers, Nursery Workers, Parents, Children, and Teens.

The opportunity is available to your church to sponsor one of these dynamic seminars. Author and speaker David Walters has been imparting a fresh vision and anointing to parents and those that work with children and youth.

- ◆ Teenagers do not have a junior Holy Spirit and children don't have a baby Holy Spirit!
- ◆ Children are not filled with the Holy Spirit for entertainment, or a couple of object lessons!
- ◆ The average church-wise child and teen can be turned around and set on fire for God!
- ◆ Christian teenagers do not have to surrender to peer pressure - they can become peers!
- ◆ Strong willed children and rebellious teenagers can become loving and obedient.

David Walters has written a number of books including, **Kids in Combat, Children Aflame, The Anointing and You, Equipping the Younger Saints, Radical Living in an Ungodly Society and 5 Children's Illustrated Bible Study books**. His articles have also appeared in many publications including Charisma and Ministries Today.

"David Walters is initiating the most awesome will of God for any specialized ministry." **- Paul Cain**

"David Walters is doing for youngsters what we are doing for adults." **- Dr. Bill Hamon**

"David Walters introduces children and youth to the power of the Holy Spirit and then trains them." **- Bob Weiner**

"David Walters is anointed to lead even the very young into moving with the gifts of the Holy Spirit" - R**oberts Liardon**

Contact to schedule a weekend or for more information

1-478-757-8071

Good News Ministries
220 Sleepy Creek Rd
Macon GA 31210

goodnews@reynoldscable.net
www.goodnews.netministries.org

Other Titles by David Walters

Kids in Combat - *Training children and youth to be powerful for God.(For parents, teachers and youth pastors)*

Equipping the Younger Saint - *Raising Godly children and teaching them spiritual gifts.*
(For parents, teachers and youth pastors)

Children Aflame - *Amazing Accounts of children from the journals of the great Methodist preacher John Wesley in the 1700's and David's own accounts with children and youth today.*

The Anointing and You - *How to bring, receive, sustain, and pass on the current renewal/revival to the next generation.*

Worship fur Dummies - *David Walters calls himself a dummy in the area of praise and worship, but he knows the ways of the Holy Spirit.*

Radical Living in a Godless Society - *Our Godless Society really targets our children and youth. How do we cope with this situation.*

Children=s Bible Studies by David Walters
(For parents, teachers, teens and children)

Armor of God - *Illustrated children's Bible study of Ephesians 6: l0 - 18. (For children ages 6-15 years)*

Fact or Fantasy? - *Illustrated children's study in Christian apologetics. (For children ages 9- 15 years)*

Being a Christian - *Illustrated children's Scripture study on being a Christian (For children ages 6-15 years)*

Fruit of the Spirit - *Illustrated children's Bible study of Gal. 5:22 & 23. (For children ages 6-15 years)*

The Gifts of the Spirit – *Children's Illustrated Bible study on the Gifts of the Spirit (ages 8-adult).*